BLAA, BLAA

C000102131

Rhymes from the Back Plot

Volume 4
in an
occasional series –

this time featuring
'Occasional' poems
from and for the
Brookfield **L**ane
Allotment **A**ssociation

Proceeds to Prostate Cancer UK

Book Information

First published in Great Britain in 2022 by Poetry Doctor Publications.

ISBN – 978-1-7391915-1-1

A collection of poems inspired by and written with great affection for the goings on at Brookfield Lane Allotment Association. Drawn mostly from life at the allotments during the 2010s, here you can find documented, in rhyme and often richly punned, a full range of garden-plot experiences. The excitement of a new noticeboard! The drama of the annual prize-giving! The regular rhythms of tending plants, maintenance rotas, upgrading of facilities – and of course, the endless war on those cabbage patch pests eager to claim the rows of vegetables as their own.

As with Phil's previous poetry books, proceeds from sales of this collection are donated:

Proceeds to Prostate Cancer UK.

Contents

Allotment, with view towards Macclesfield, 2010

BLAA, BLAA, Black Sheep

BLAA, BLAA*, Black Sheep,
      have you any weeds?
Yes, sir, yes, sir, all gone to seeds:
some for our Casey, some for our Dave,
and some for Big Bob
      and the rest of Brookfield Lane.

** The poems in this collection are inspired by
involvement with the **Brookfield Lane Allotment
Association** and seek above all to celebrate the hard
work at and for the Association by Dave 'Casey' Jones,
Dave Hodgkiss and our valiant band of volunteers.*

Party Time at Brookfield Allotment

Guy 'Forks' Night, November 13th, 2010

The minutes of the AGM
contained this year a little gem:
'Upon a certain day convened,
a working party, gloved and jeaned,
will undertake to dig a trench'
(thus working up a thirst to quench),
'replacing furred up water pipes,
improving flow whilst stemming gripes'.

Then someone had a bright idea:
'It coincides this time of year,
and though it's not *our* kind of plot,
let's celebrate Guy Fawkes. Why not?'
So, on a dark November day,
with maintenance got out the way
discreetly by the usual crew,
the many joined the worthy few.

Marquees were raised. The path was lit.
The many all chipped in a bit.
On folding tables, food was spread:
Pat-ato pies and Parkin bread.

Allotment 'taters' in their foil
just brushed with barbie baking oil,
with chestnuts, ready for the grill
and skewered kebabs the throng to fill.

And drink? Let it not be forgot
those stoking fires get really hot.
A brazier à la picket line
is thirsty work, deserves mulled wine,
bottled cider and cans of beer
(just some of what's on offer here)
and downed with great alacrity,
though someone claimed they preferred tea!

The time arrived for bonfire-ette
with Health and Safety in a sweat.
Twigs sputtered, smoked. The flame expired,
then cardboard gave the end desired.
Meanwhile, a fearless pair prepared
firework display, the perils shared:
Roman Candle and Traffic Light
an instant lit the Brookfield night.

A torch was needed from the shed
passed hanging lantern. 'Mind your head!'
Too late. More stars. You feel a Charlie.
Quick, move on to grand finale.
Launch tube in place, touch paper fizzed,
heavenward, up the rocket whizzed.
One mighty bang, a flash, then stars,
brought forth the chorused 'oohs' and 'aahs'.

So, time for home. Well, one last drink,
and though the plastic cups don't chink,
a toast was made to rousing cheer:
'Here's to the crops we grow next year'.
A plaintive voice, perhaps to tease,
said, 'Can I have the wood ash, please?'
Thus replacing pipes and socket
led from little gem to rocket.

The Chard of the Brookfield Spade

With apple juice to Alfred Lord Tennyson

Thirty leeks, forty leeks,
fifty leeks upwards,
all in the allotment earth,
rows by the hundred.
'Forward the Brookfield Spade!
Chard for the greens!' they said.
Into the allotment earth,
rows by the hundred.

'Forward the Brookfield Spade!'
Was there a man dismayed?
Not though the gardeners knew
someone had blundered.

Theirs not to make reply.
Theirs not to reason why.
Theirs but to hoe and try
into the allotment earth,
rows by the hundred.

Carrots to the right of them,
carrots to the left of them,
carrots in front of them,
caulis in hundreds;

storms before sunny spell.
Boldly their rows did swell,
into the fertile earth,
on top the mulch as well,
rows by the hundred.

Flashed all their spades in toil,
flashed as they turned the soil,
hearing the kettle boil,
char drinking army, while
all the world wondered.

Pausing to share a joke,
mainly they're local folk
from Macc and Sutton,
heads up high, hearts of oak,
hatted and sun-dried.

When can their story fade?
O, the Swiss chard they made!
All the world wondered.
And the courgettes they made!
Honour the Brookfield Spade,
all this unfunded.

Frenzy

or, Where There's Muck, There's Brassica*

The delivery arrived in the morning
when the load was expected and planned
and some took to heart the forewarning
and made sure that their garden was manned.

The pile had had scarce time to settle.
Wisps of steam were just starting to rise.
Each gardener was put on his mettle,
actions springing from words to the wise.

Each was armed with fork, sacks and barrow,
these zealots who were first on the scene,
disappearing up paths long and narrow.
The heap visibly shrank where they'd been.

They stuck to their task with a vigour.
Six barrowsful was the quota assigned,
though whether applied with a rigour,
let's just say I've an eye which is blind.

Like a shimmering mirage in heat haze
or a liquid spread out in the sun,
one minute a towering hill's in your gaze,
you blink twice and the next it has gone.

The dung beetle's known for its penchant,
gathering up what it treats as pure gold,
ignoring what others may think of the stench and
trundling it off before it grows cold.

We've a similar outlook, we gardeners.
We see value in animal waste.
Gung-ho with dung, O don't be too hard on us.
Our produce will be a bit more to your taste.

* Poetic licence: in fact, manure is best avoided for the brassica bed.

Allotment Year

As wisps of night evaporate
       and teetering gate posts lurch,
upon the highest greenhouse roof,
       the blackbird claims his perch.
Another early bird's arrived
       and startled pigeons flap.
A gardener's here to plant his crops
       before mid-morning nap.

He's done his preparation and replenished tired soil,
manure and compost double dug
       will soon reward his toil.
Desultory prods with trowels made,
       it's time to have a brew
and sit and sip and sip and sit
       and watch the shoots break through.

Returning sun has warmed the ground.
       Some rocket's gone to seed.
Inspection day will soon be round.
       He clears his plot of weed,
but almost as he watches, they're thrusting up again.
He scores the same as last year, only seven out of ten.

There are subtle, precious pleasures
        that come with Grow-Your-Own:
there's how to judge the seasons;
        there's how to spell home 'groan';
there's the taste of new potatoes
        freshly lifted from the ground;
and he's no need of sunbed hire,
        he's organically browned.

Then once a year, he has the chance
        to show in head-to-head
the produce of his gardening skills
        from each and every bed,
and, not at all contrary,
        prove how cherished gardens grow
and chant that age old mantra:
        'Dig, plant, pick your crops and go'.

Slugging It Out in No Man's Land

The twilight hour: it's now or never;
over the top and time to attack.
The terrain's wet. It's perfect weather.
We'll hit them hard and set off back.

The light is fading. Switch head torch on;
weapons are ready and so are we.
We'll hunt them down till we've left none.
Then home to bed with the plot slug free.

Between you and me,
unfortunately,
this is a very,
temporary
valedictory
pseudo-victory.

The Gardener's Butterfly Prayer

O God, all-seeing, who is wise,
I love all graceful butterflies.
They float and feint and pose and rise;
each dart which gravity defies
an unpredictable surprise.
They are free spirits in disguise:
a balm, a lotion for the eyes.
Their wafting flight all sense denies.
Although diminutive in size,
of airborne insects, they're the prize.
(Think aphids, midges, wasps and flies).

O God, who all our sins espies,
ignore this guff, this pack of lies
for cabbage whites I just despise.
One cannot bear them, though one tries,
rejoicing when their species dies.
Why they exist reason defies.
I plot to bring on their demise.
You will not stop me with your sighs
or tempting me with thoughts of thighs.
I wish it could be otherwise,
I must, alas, prioritise.

O God, please help me fight the fight.
Yes, I despise the cabbage white.
Exterminate the little shite.
They seem to take such great delight
when on my sprouts and greens alight
and though they dance and twirl in flight,
for me they are a dreadful blight
upon the earth, so much I might
take measures to resolve my plight:
invent a gadget causing fright;
robotic arm which swipes from height;
train some insectivores to bite;
or build some traps which squeeze them tight.
I wouldn't be the least contrite
for the reaction they incite.
It's evil, yes, for it's not right
on helpless bugs to vent one's spite.
Alas, this is a qualm so slight
I try to kill all those in sight.
I'd work until it's almost night
to clear the last one from our site.
Perhaps the future would be bright
if they could join the trilobite,
a specimen by Araldite®

fixed on a slide like lymphocyte
and viewed by a revealing light
by pupil, prof. or acolyte,
a thing of study recondite.

O, God, destroy the cabbage white!

Amen.

Elephant Hawk Moth Caterpillar

It is a magnificent monster:
fully three inches long, half an inch wide,
It lies prone on the compost bag,
where it had fallen, like a wingless Icarus,
singed by the rays from the fuschia's purple suns.
A parcel of hawk moth DNA, grey and green,
segmented,
its *eyes* and *horns* confuse, confound and combine
to repel the passing predator.

Ready for transition and pupal transformation,
ready for that avian mother with her ravenous brood,
it's special, yet not 'Today's Special',
not the next morsel on the menu.
It adopts defensive posture,
the snake or elephant imposture.

Undeterred, I pick it up and
drop it gingerly on to the grass in the jar,
a temporary trophy for identification.
Its past had been fuschia,
its future a chrysalis cocooned,
before the final turn in the life cycle's wheel
opens its flight path back home at last
to the kingdom of the heavens.

The Dig Society

When Adam delved and Eve span,
each chipped in and no-one ran
for Parliament.

           Then some toff thought
'It's time these oicks woke up. They ought
to show more drive, more fire, ambition.
They need a me, a politician,
someone to lead them from the fore,
to take the helm in time of war.'

And Eve span on whilst Adam delved.
They'd had their mutual future shelved.
Instead, there was a Five year Plan
to which they both toiled to a man
to build a 'Big Society'
(a phrase pronounced with piety),

but let's be clear, the toil was theirs,
whilst benefits went in equal shares,
though of course some shares more equal.
'Animal Farm', the natural sequel,

analysed the operation,
satirised the situation,
deconstructed, brick by brick:
the progress slow; the profit quick.

The 'Big Society'? Oh, Big Brother,
with half a choice, I'd choose the other.

And this is the way the world ends,
and this is the way the world ends,
and this is the way the world ends,
a 'Big Society', my friends.

Weeds

We've lost an art, a vanished skill
and I blame Wordsworth's daffodil.
For way back in the mists of Rhyme
(before we feared a change of clime),
the medieval gardener,
the scullion and the pardoner,
each had a sacred, secret way
of keeping fruit and veg at bay.

They coaxed and nurtured, fed and nourished
weeds – yes, weeds – until they flourished.
They couldn't get enough of them,
eradicated Little Gem,
ensured that such unwanted guests,
like beetroot, chard and other pests,
were short shrift given and rooted out
or slowly killed by endless drought.

They aimed to grow the perfect weed
which from invasive veg was freed.
Of bean-less, pea-less fields they dreamt,
of gardens, overrun, unkempt,

knee deep in three- and four-leafed clover
from Scottish Isles to east of Dover.

Ever alert and on their mettle,
they strove to grow the stinging nettle,
alongside plantain, thistle, dock,
blew seeds of dandelion clock.
(In French it's known as pisse-en-lit
for diuretic property!)

These days I seem to be alone,
encouraging the weeds I've sown.
My fellow gardeners to a man
despise the knot weed from Japan,
care not for Himalayan balsam
whose blossoms I consider wholesome.

If these or ragwort you have none,
it's me you need, not Monty Don.

To Marrow and To Marrow and To Marrow…

With apologies to 'O Sole Mio', 'It's Now or Never' and
'Just One Cornetto'

Just one courgetto. Give it to me.
It's called *zucchini** in Italy.
To marrow, if we're too late,
it's now or never, so please don't wait.

When I first saw it
with its flesh so tender,
my heart was captured,
my soul surrendered.
I'd spend a lifetime
waiting for the ripe time.
Now that it's near,
the time is here at last.

Just one courgetto. Give it to me.
It's called *zucchini* in Italy.
To marrow, if we're too late,
it's now or never, our stove won't wait.

*And, um, in American English, too, of course.

Garden Share

If gardens that you rent or own
are underused and overgrown,
if your work is too demanding,
if your family's expanding,
or if your fingers just aren't green
(and you prefer to keep them clean),
or if you have no time to spare
to tend it, why not garden share?
If you find digging's far too hard,
you'd rather sunbathe in your yard,
we'll pair you up with volunteers.
You'll then have veg without the tears
for willingly the spade work's done
by folk who find it rather fun.
They'll work the soil and plant the veg.
with honest toil they make this pledge:
'Let's share the crops so we all gain.
That's good, today it looks like rain'.

End-of -Season Rites

Early November
and the greenhouse glass drips with condensation.
'Sunbabies' dangle, little yellow baubles on their vines,
still somehow bringing sweetness and a touch of colour,
a foretaste of the festivities to come.
Flowerpots, in disarray under the potting bench,
tumble together like the discarded leaves outside.
Soil-caked, half-forgotten tools prepare to hibernate
and I'm alone with the mature, yellowing plants,
alone except for snails, munching, munching, munching,
but the sound I hear is Winter creeping across the plot,
stalking the last of the lettuce,
making the cream cones of parsnip syrup sweet.

I watch the sun setting above the far townscape.
It glints wanly on the slate roofs and aerials,
but turns the clouds the reds of holly berries,
of 'Gardener's Delight' and that cheeky, perching robin.
Head cocked, is he singing for me?
Or for his young long flown the nest?
Or to charm those juicy worms from their clay domain,
a year's end feast to take him through to better times?

Eric Bloodaxe?

He was quiet and introverted. A nod would just suffice.
He minded his own business, wouldn't pry at any price.
He nurtured his allotment plot with tender loving care,
but sometimes you might catch him
      with a far off, wistful stare.

He'd sit down with his mug of tea,
      well-earned mid-morning break,
or pause from planting labours
      and lean hard upon his rake.
His head would fill with images that frankly he deplored.
He had no explanation
      as shrill noises howled and roared.

It seemed he manned a long boat oar
      with rough and calloused hands.
He'd crossed the sea at risk of life
      to reach these hostile lands.
He wore a Viking helmet, by his side his trusty axe,
which hung there at the ready
      till he reached their squalid shacks.

Blood-curdling oaths he'd utter
        as he lashed out left and right.
He never gave a second thought,
        just hacked with all his might
and speed was of the essence
        ere the men folk would return:
seize what they could,
        then back to sea and leave the huts to burn.

Were Eric's ancestral voices an echo from his genes?
He mulled this concept over
        as he hoed his peas and beans.
These days he rakes and tillages.
        It's spuds that he will sack
and only in odd moments DNA will draw him back.

The distant past lies buried
        and long gone those roving bands.
Nowadays, blood, fish and bone meal,
        it is on Eric's hands.
So, pass the time of day with him,
        then leave him to his work.
For there's the faintest, outside chance
        that Eric'll go berserk.

Casey's Gate

I've written poems on gardening themes:
there's 'Eric Bloodaxe?', lost in dreams;
there's one I called 'Allotment Dawn';
one cursed why cabbage whites were born;
another told when frenzied dash
for horse manure caused quite a clash –

And skits: 'Chard of The Brookfield Spade';
'Just One Courgetto' serenade;
and Guy 'Forks' night in 2010.
Blow me! It's time to write again.

'The reason is', I hear him say,
in soothing burr from Gloucester way,
'it wun't be right to quite ignore
the fact. That's wha' you poets are for.'

So, let me tell you of the state
that's led to Casey's brand new gate.
The one we had with chain and lock
the slightest breeze would shake and rock.

Its fragile structure so vibrated,
replacement was investigated.
Cometh the hour, cometh the man.
T'committee formed a cunning plan.

'That gate will fall on some young kid'.
Prophetic words. It almost did.
So urgent action was required
by someone overall attired.
They scratched their heads. 'Who could it be?'
In unison, they cried, 'Casey'.

To Casey they then turned to ask
if he'd take on this mammoth task.
He thought a second, then replied,
'Your faith in me can't be denied.
I'll do it, friends. Leave it to me
and we shall see what we shall see'.

The next weekend, it scarcely rained.
A certain man the gate unchained,
from trusty van his tools removed,

laid out his plan, as is approved
and noted distances and angles,
once his tape measure disentangles.

With knitted brows and maledictions,
he calculated space restrictions,
marked out where the gate would swing
by using lengths of twine and string.
All that remained in line of duty?
Arrange delivery of the beauty.

Two stalwart wooden posts were bought,
essential items to support
the metal framework and the grill.
The treasurer asked to see the bill,
paled visibly and clutched his chest,
a deep sigh heaved. 'Well, you know best'.

So Casey delved, then dug some more.
Great mounds of soil upon the floor
rose up towards the hills and sky
and stood at least 2 metres high.

Cement was bought. Cement was mixed,
poured into holes and posts affixed.
On 25th. of Jan. was hung
the gate whose praises I have sung.

On top and on each side stood proud
that grill to stop those not allowed
from climbing over, breaking in.
Job done! My, didn't our Casey grin.

So, gone old, rickety disgrace,
a spanking new one in its place.
All that remains (the fame is his):
to christen 'Casey's Gate' with fizz.

Come On, Casey, Right What's Dire

I'm not on Facebook, not on Twitter,
so could it have been a ghost
for – fellow gardeners, please don't titter –
The Doors have sent me this new post?

'We know that what we say is true.
We know that we are not a liar.
If they stop to have a brew,
well, it's 'cos their throats are drier.

Come on, Casey, right what's dire.
Come on, Casey, right what's dire.
To keep the roof up, please aspire.

The time to hesitate is through.
Just time to swallow and admire.
Later you can sup some booze,
once you've found an oak supplier.

Come on, Casey, right what's dire.
Come on, Casey, right what's dire.
To keep the roof up, please aspire.'

And so it was that crumbling post
by Casey, Dave and Keith was smashed
and as they are not ones to boast,
I must make sure the news is splashed.

They've sweated blood (and fish and bone),
installed a doorpost made from oaks.
They did all that with scarce a groan.
That's what I call 'Allotment blokes'.

So, lads, put on your best attire
take it easy and respire.
We'll publicise it in Cheshire,
circulate it on a flyer,
get it shouted by Town Crier.

So, Dave and Keith, you both inspire.
and 'Thank You', Casey Jones, esquire.

Dave and Casey: Pen Portraits

You've heard me go on, sometimes at great length
about Dave and Casey, our backbone, our strength,
but now my friend Margaret has asked to know more
and a plea for pen portraits I just can't ignore.

Take Casey:
He's jovial, he's genial, a jack of all trades
and an absolute must for allotment upgrades.
An ex-lorry driver, just like his dad,
but he's long since retired and Life's not that bad.

He's 'big-boned' and stocky, you couldn't say lean,
with an ear-soothing burr from the Forest of Dean.

His overall's blue and essential for tasks
for it's praises, not sunshine, in which he basks.
His grey thatch is cropped short above that broad smile,
a wise and bespectacled *allotmentophile*.

Whilst Dave, ex-accountant, is also retired,
he's staunch and reliable, widely admired.
On the tall side of medium, grey haired with specs.
and often involved in inspections and checks.

From somewhere near Bolton, a Wanderers' fan,
a reliant Robin to Casey's Batman.

He's thoughtful, reflective, gives sound advice,
has a wry sense of humour. He's pleasant. He's 'nice'.
His accent is northern, of that there's no doubt,
Need compost or pellets? Just give him a shout.

With his faithful dog stretched out at his feet
and wife, Pam, at his side, the picture's complete.

Casey (& Co.)'s Roof

When gardeners come to Brookfield Lane
on days it happens not to rain,
they will have noticed recently
Casey and friends sat drinking tea,
delicious brew supplied by Pat,

which begs the question, 'Why is that?'
Don't be deceived. These lads don't shirk.
It's just a pause. They're hard at work.

This time the roof of shed-cum-shop
hung by a thread about to drop,
obliterating those inside
and risking gardener homicide.

So those who may anticipate
a follow-up to 'Casey's Gate',
sit back whilst I relate my tale
(also available in Braille).
How handy is our shed-cum-shop!
To buy our compost in we pop

and, queuing up in single file,
there's even service with a smile.
Our credit's good, but we pay cash
for pellets, lime, bone meal, potash.
And so, it came as quite a shock
when leaky roof attacked the stock.

The dreadful news like wildfire spread.
Matters came quickly to a head.
Committee members met and frowned.
'We mustn't see our assets drowned.
Let's formulate an action plan.
As with that gate, Casey's our man.
To help he'll need a hand-picked crew,
(though almost anyone will do).

Step 1: dismantle rotten roof.
Step 2: make new one weatherproof.
Between Steps 1 and 2, Step 3:
make sure they don't run out of tea.'
Now Dave had recently retired
and in a flash found himself hired
and as his job he'd called a halt on
he gave a hand the roof to **BOLT ON***.

Another vital wheel in t'cog,
was John man and his faithful dog.
John's canine chum would stand on guard
ensuring no-one worked too hard
and so that it went smooth and slick,
our volunteers co-opted Mick.
One final ploy: Facebook appeal
for more to come and share their zeal.

On the day, the gang assembled,
joists and rafters creaked and trembled.
The day of reckoning was nigh,
with blazing sun, the pressure high
and omens good for such a task,
a day more fit to bronze and bask.
But first things first, the dirty bit:
demolish roof and curse and spit.

The valiant crew began to sweat,
their overalls showed patches wet
and throats were parched whilst foreheads dripped.
How come their morale hadn't dipped?

Thanks to Pat's kind ministrations,
meriting standing ovations,
a constant flow of tea they downed
with water for John's faithful hound.

That night when daylight's glow had fled,
 the precious stock in shop-cum-shed
was sheltered by a sturdy sheet,
protecting heaped up sacks of peat.
The blue tarpaulin firmly roped
with breeze and prowlers amply coped.
Now to the step requiring strength:
lift roof board cut to measured length.

Somehow our men in sapping heat
achieved this Herculean feat.
They pulled and puffed. It slowly rose
to where it was destined to pose.
At times, all four were up aloft.
This was no task for someone soft
or suffering from vertigo.
To heroes this new roof we owe.

Enough, my friends, it now remains
when you call in for bamboo canes,
to gaze, admire their work of art
and know that it came from the heart.
So, there I'll end and draw a veil,
round off this warm, uplifting tale.
Forgive if I have waffled on
about Dave, Casey, Mick and John.

Let's raise the roof for Casey's saga:
three rousing cheers and pints of lager.

* Dave is an avid fan of Bolton Wanderers.

New Noticeboard

At Brookfield Lane, we're flush with cash.
It's that or we're being rather rash,
'cos first that old gate was replaced,
then shop or shed with new roof graced,
plus doorpost and a lick of paint.
(So, 'Thank you, Casey, you're a saint').

That must be all we can afford.
Blow me, a brand new noticeboard
appears and boy, is it a whopper!
I swear it's filigreed with copper.
It's more impressive and ornate
and flash than aforementioned gate.

Next to the shed as bold as brass,
equipped with tinted, toughened glass,
ordered from a posh magazine:
The Chairman's Giant TV Screen.
(I bet for just another tenner,
they would have thrown in an antenna.)

Now, if I could, as dusk was nearing,
pull up my chair and begin peering,
I'm sure that I could watch unfurl(ed)
that Monty Don and Gardener's World
and Simon Mayo's The Big Dig.
For Carol Klein, I'd do a jig,

and, though not wishing to be harsh,
I'd switch off quick one A. Titchmarsh.
Alas, the board's not electronic.
To tell the truth, not even sonic.
Though every penny it is worth,
its major virtue is its girth!

Dave and Casey

If you call at our allotment and wonder how we keep
the place so neat and tidy, it's 2 men who never sleep.
They're constantly on duty if appearances are right
and I reckon that they sometimes
      even camp there overnight.
You will not need three guesses
      to name these fine, upstanding men.
It's Dave and Casey, Siamese twins.
      You'll find them in their den.

They've overhauled the bunker
      and they've built a new raised bed.
They laid the bricks and mortar
      till the poor sods' fingers bled.
They filled it up with topsoil
      and Dave's wife did the rest.
With marigolds and dahlias
      and tomatoes we're now blessed.
The shop front was quite grotty,
      so they took the time to pave
with slabs and stone one of them sourced.
      Was it Casey or our Dave?

You'll have seen them trimming hedges
       and carting to the tip
every leaf and twig and branch they were obliged to clip.
They gathered up scrap metal
       which had lain around the patch
and flogged it off at Henshaw's
       who found he'd met his match
for Casey bargained for best price.
       He had Henshaw in tears,
but with that Glo'ster burr he said,
       'Thanks very much, my dears.'

They've seeded near the raised bed
       to give that crowning touch.
They're running out of projects.
       At straws they'll start to clutch.
Perhaps we're overdue a bar
       where we could quench our thirst,
once weeding duties over. It would likely be a first.
One thing is sure and certain.
       We don't need a sauna or a gym.
We dig at speed and hoe and weed
       to keep ourselves in trim.

And now I've sung their praises
       in these verses sweet and short.
I speak for every one of us in offering our support.
 So, when you see them in the shop,
       tidying up those nooks,
buy your compost bags and smile
       and maybe buy my books*!
Keep up the good work, Casey.
       Dave, don't **Wander**** off too far.
What a brilliant partnership!
       Let's just end with one big 'Ta!'

** Unashamed plug for 'Eric Bloodaxe? And Other Verse', 'Seconds Out', 'Lifelines' and 'BLAA, BLAA, Black Sheep'. As with all my poetry booklets, proceeds go to **Prostate Cancer UK.***

**As mentioned, Dave is a keen Bolton Wanderers fan.

Working Party Time

Not another bloomin' ditty
      from that bloomin' Poyser bloke.
You can't sneeze up here without some verse.
      It's getting past a joke.

October 10th. we'd mobilised
      the Autumn working party
with every chance we'd finish up
      all sweaty, tired and clarty.
At 10 o'clock, we've got stuck in
      with tasks explained to t'work force,
with Mick's lot at the far end
      where Casey's bantering till he's hoarse,
whilst Dave's team clears hedge cuttings
      from a plot that's overgrown
along with Graham the Treasurer,
      so not quite on his own.

Then Phil polls up and joins them
      to shred trimmings for the tip
and it takes a good 10 minutes
      ere Dave has to crack the whip.

They're chatting about cricket, Brexit,
       what crops have failed this year
and just how long it seems till t'break
       and will there be some beer.

But somehow Dave's trailer gets filled
       right to the brim and cuttings stashed,
but there's lots of work remains to do
       before the tea gets mashed.
It's like those digs you see with Tony Robinson on TV
except it's much more frenzied,
       barrows buzzing past you – one – two – three.

There's Maggie with a shovel shifting shavings in a blur
and Mick, Big Bob and Jane's mum
       struggling to keep pace with her.
It's a triumph for our teamwork
       and when the dust cloud clears,
the space is rough and ready,
       gone accumulation of the years.
So, the chips are down or rather up,
       sweats trickling down our backs.
A kettle's boiling on the grill
       between the sheds and shacks.

The tea is brewed.

      It's sipped and slurped with great enthusiasm.
and more than one of us seize up
      with cramp and muscle spasm.

Sausage rolls we scoff and sponge cake
      worthy of 'Great British Bake Off'
and we're a little bit rebellious
      when it comes to t'time to break off,
but back we go to finish off the task we have in hand
knowing our allotment site's improved.
      It surely will be grand,
but one of us has lost the plot or rather lost his keys
and spends the next two days
      around the site upon his knees.
Phil's fervent prayers are granted
      just as all hope's begun to fade.
They're found at home in Mady's bag!
      Not lost, merely M/s-laid.

Just 2 more lines still to recite,
      then I'll get back to my beer:
That sponge cake! Those sausage rolls!
      When's working party time next year?

The Day That the (D)Rains Came Down (Up)

Whenever problems rear their heads
amongst our vegetable beds,
at Brookfield Lane ideas are stormed
and working parties duly formed.
It came to pass our water pipes
caused much concern, comments and snipes:

those made of lead must be replaced
(a thorn to tackle with some haste);
a lack of pressure; taps that leaked;
the system struggled, groaned and creaked,
so, time to boldly grasp the nettle,
this project which would test our mettle.

As Autumn leaves were turning brown
and cultivation winding down,
October's last weekend was picked,
pre-Hallowe'en, pre-treat-or-trick-ed,
before Jack Frost could turn to stone
the earth and chill us to the bone.

The nights draw in and soon it's dark,
but we're in luck, for we have Mark
with all his years with Cheshire Water,
he'll galvanise every supporter.
He'll head the project, organise it.
Casey and Dave will advertise it.

On Friday, the first work began,
equipped with high vis. vests each man,
ear plugs and protective goggles
for Bob who drill and digger joggles
and cordoned off with canes and tape
the areas where trench would gape.

The weather was to say the least
a stormy, angry, monsoon beast.
The rain lashed down upon our men.
On Saturday: the same again.
Where we had dug the water rose
and caused all sorts of aqueous woes.

We felt like Noah in the flood
without his ark. No bloody good.
Our work force, soaked and mud-bespattered
the furious elements had battered.
At 3 o'clock, we almost cheered –
the clouds rolled back, the sun appeared.

From time to time, we paused for breaks.
A brew was served with scones and cakes.
At lunch, hot pies and sausage rolls
sustained the hungry troops. More holes
were dug and the pipeline threaded.
At last, we saw where we were headed.

Phil'd had an op for cataract
so mainly watched, drank tea and snacked.
One useful role that Casey hatched:
with petrol cans Phil was despatched.
He went with three, but filled just two,
as new law limits what you do.

The clocks went back, and Sunday dawned,
More volunteers all stretched and yawned
and then they dug with renewed vigour
with pick and shovel and the digger.
A luncheon stew was cooked by Pat
with Pam's soup for starters prior to that.

They toiled away all afternoon
until upon the ground was strewn
great beads of sweat to join the pools
which threatened to engulf their tools.
When Monday came, the job was done,
followed by heavy frost and sun.

So, thanks to all who played their part
to make the system state of art.
That's Dennis, Nigel, Ian, 2 Petes,
and Roger with his homemade sweets,
(cream, jam and scones, 2 apple pies,
so good they well deserved a prize),

Keith, Alan, Martin, Simon, Andy
(I'll put him last. The rhyme is handy).
You have to say that's quite a list,
but is there anyone I've missed?
Well, Dave and Casey, Bob and Mick,
who all through thick and thin did stick.

And last of all, but not the least,
our ladies who ensured the feast:
that's Lizzie, Naomi, Pat, Sue, Pam
plus, Helen, Emily and Kate.
Excuse my French, *mais, ouf, quelles femmes!*
I'll tiptoe out and close the gate.

Brookfield Lane Allotment Show

Twentieth of August, and I have to go.
It's time for Brookfield Lane Allotment Show.
We plot holders gathered here at St. Paul's,
this morning brought entries and set out our stalls
to display this year's produce and show our prowess.
(Who the winners will be isn't too hard to guess).
Courgettes, beans, carrots, the perfect sweet pea:
I'm just taking part. It's clearly not me!
Jellies and jams, maybe in with a shout,
but participation is what it's about.

Those cakes! They're to die for. Bring on the auction.
My sweet tooth says, 'Buy me at least one concoction'.
But before we get round to making our bids,
the judge reads the winners, grown-ups and kids
and finishing off with a quiz and a raffle.
(It's a bottle of wine I'm hoping to snaffle)
Then one final highlight to round off the Show:
Pat's famous hot pie of meat and potato.
Jane, Mick and Graham, Bob, Casey and John:
a big thanks to you all! Another year gone!

The Blackberry Jam Scandal

It's been quite a while since I wrote you an ode
on Brookfield Allotment and what our folk showed
and which veg won prizes and whose faces glowed
a whole year ago at the annual fête.
I've written of noticeboards, shop roof and gate –
so, it's time that I gave you another update.

Well, next to the flower bed, we now have a bench.
You can sit – if you've time – at the risk of a drench,
with plenty of room for yourself and your wench.
It's raised on a platform of stout paving stones,
assembled by Dave and, of course, Casey Jones
and what better place to play *Game of Thrones*.

That flower bed is worthy of prizes at Tatton.
You get a good view from the bench that you're sat on
unless garden fatigue has you lying out flat on.
There are dahlias with heads as big as a plate,
creeping nasturtiums that are good when they're 'ate'
and too many others for me to relate.

And this year's show was a roaring success.
Now I'll come to my title which I should address
and my lack of first prizes which caused some distress*.
With *Single Sweet Pea*, I walked off with second prize.
There were at least three exhibits. I tell you no lies,
but it's on jams and jellies that I'd set my eyes.

Two jars of each I entered, hoping not to be bested,
but these categories were hotly contested.
and it's only now my disappointment has festered.
The white currant jelly was a bit out of left field
and the red currant sadly was scarcely congealed.
My first jam – nothing – for imminent failure I steeled.

With blackberry jam unopened, my Fate was sealed.
Perhaps I was unlucky. Maybe it was the gamble
of mislabelling the d$mn thing, blackberry, not bramble?

Not really!

Cutey Rooty

Carrot divine! Carrot of mine!
O, will you be my Valentine?

When first I teased you from your bed,
how my pulse raced! My face went red,
not that vermilion, perfect hue
defines your beauty through and through,
but splodgy-cheeked, like naughty child.
I was transfixed, lovelorn, beguiled.
For though I knew that you'd been culled,
at last, my love, at least I'd pulled.

Staring thus, not calm nor manic,
gazing on your form organic,
your head, adorned with feathery fronds
a vibrant green (Who cares for blondes?),
I bathed your body in its prime
to clean away the surface grime.
No pestilence, no carrot fly,
had marred you with invasion sly.

At home, my love, it's time to dine
and share a sumptuous meal divine.
First, I remove your outer dress
and tenderly your shape caress,
your inner self, your flesh reveal.
You hit the spot, that's X-appeal.
And so we face the final crunch:
to eat you now or wait for lunch?

Carrot divine! Carrot of mine!
O, will you be my Valentine?

First Prize in the Cute-cumber Category

I can't let this pass without comment in rhyme
Fly flags. Hang out bunting.
      Let's hear church bells chime.
My big day had come. I'd been waiting for years.
I'm feeling emotional, almost in tears.
For Saturday last was the day of the Show.
We hopefuls turned up with our produce in tow.
30 p for each entry, so serious stuff,
and winning first prizes would be really tough.

Whether single sweet pea or trios of veg.,
how would we find that competitive edge?

The morning past quickly selecting our crops,
the pick of the bunch. There'd be no room for flops:
a monster tomato; 3 beetroot; 3 beans;
a white, frilly squash; and maybe some greens;
one pot of marmalade; one pot of bramble;
one rhubarb and ginger (a bit of a gamble).
and one final entry, last but not least,
an arrow straight cucumber, fit for a feast.

On the stroke of midday, the judging began,
Would the afternoon go according to plan?

3 o'clock soon came round. We scurried back in,
eager to see who had managed to win.
Laid out on the tables, the results were displayed.
Had any of my entries made the grade?
Yes, here I'd a third prize, there I'd a second.
That was lots more success than I'd reckoned.
The sponges and scones I sauntered right past
and headed for where the cucurbits amassed

and I swear that this all logic defies,
there was my cucumber sporting first prize.

'Yippee!', I shouted, though just in my head.
(Showing you've triumphed is very ill-bred).
It wasn't the longest. It wasn't its size.
It wasn't its girth that won it first prize,
but somehow it embodied perfection:
most rectilinear in the cucumber section.
Its skin satin smooth, a beautiful green,
a tiny bit shiny which gave it a sheen.

I'm over the moon. I'm chuffed as can be.
Maybe next year, 'Best in Show' might be me!

Acknowledgements

First and foremost is Mady, who has managed to put up with me for three decades, through thick and thin, in full time employment and in retirement and even whilst I was in the throes of getting something resembling the right words in something resembling the right order.

Sincere thanks are also due to Chris Cottom who has taken time to read this text and give me feedback. Any remaining errors and idiosyncrasies of layout, punctuation, etc. are my own (or my daughter's!).

Speaking of whom, my daughter, Paula Aamli, herself a sometimes-poet, has supported me by preparing this collection for publication.

My thanks also to my poetry teacher Rosanna McGlone, who through years of Poetry Appreciation classes has striven to expand my familiarity with contemporary poetry and extend the range of technical tricks and skills available to me. None of this is your fault!

Recognition of the part Macclesfield Creative Writing Group has played in supporting and encouraging me cannot be overstated. Our workshops (Macclesfield Library, Thursdays 2 to 4 pm) are a particular source of stimulation.

Finally, a word of thanks to the devotees of the *open mic* nights at which many of these poems have been read, including at 'Poems and Pints', Button Warehouse, Macclesfield; 'Write and Release', New Mills; 'Petersgate Tap', Stockport; and so on. Much is owed, as you have – perhaps unintentionally – encouraged this author by your enthusiastic response to these readings.

About the Poet

Coming from Nottinghamshire mining stock, Phil Poyser's migration from Mansfield to Macclesfield may seem little more than a minor orthographical change, but it covers a period of over half a century.

Secondary education at the Brunts Grammar School in the late 50s & early 60s was followed by B.Sc. and Ph. D. degrees at Imperial College, London, separated by a gap year travelling overland to Australia (and back) with fellow college dropout, Derek Price.

Post-doctoral research in Concepción, Chile and Strasbourg, France was a prelude to a career as a medicinal chemist in the pharmaceutical industry, firstly in Reims, France and latterly at Alderley Park, Cheshire as ICI Pharmaceuticals evolved into Zeneca Pharmaceuticals and AstraZeneca.

Retirement, or more accurately redundancy, in July, 2007 at last provided the opportunity for Phil to expand his lifelong interest in poetry and led to the publication of two small collections: 'Eric Bloodaxe? And Other Verse' (2014) and 'Seconds Out' (2016). These were well-received, with proceeds going to Prostate Cancer UK.

Poetry continues to be Phil's driving passion and – although delayed by COVID-19 lockdowns and other excursions into the care of the NHS – new selections of works generated by Phil's poetry habit are now available in two further collections, *'Lifelines'* and *'BLAA, BLAA, Black Sheep'* (both released Autumn 2022).

Along with writing and performing his poems, Phil's personal ABC (allotment, bridge and cycling) complete a packed weekly programme.

In terms of prior publication of these pieces –

'Eric Bloodaxe?' first appeared in the pamphlet bearing his name, *'Eric Bloodaxe? And Other Verse',* as did 'Allotment Year'.

Additionally, the following seven poems also feature in the pamphlet, *'Lifelines':* 'Frenzy'; 'Slugging It Out in No Man's Land'; 'The Gardener's Butterfly Prayer'; 'Casey (& Co)'s Roof'; 'Dave and Casey'; 'Working Party Time'; and 'The Blackberry Jam Scandal'.

Praise for BLAA BLAA Black Sheep

Sometimes mischievous, usually wry, but always affectionate, Phil Poyser's new collection, 'BLAA. BLAA, Black Sheep' is a delightful portrait of Little England.

> ~ Chris Cottom, Winner of the 2021 Retreat West Flash Fiction Prize

Phil Poyser, wordsmith extraordinaire, has assembled a veritable stir fry of poetry from the allotment.

Where else would you find a nod to Shakespeare paired with a well-known ice cream advertisement, than in his To Marrow poem with its 'Just One Courgetto' refrain?

Educational and humorous. If you dig poetry – and allotments – then this is the anthology for you!

> ~ Rosanna McGlone, writer, playwright ('We Are the Docks'), workshop facilitator, and former freelance journalist for The Guardian, The Independent, The Australian and The Sydney Morning Herald.

More about Phil's Poetry Here

Phil Poyser has been described as 'Cheshire's leading comic poet' (Charlie Heathcote, author of the four books in the 'Our Doris' series).

You can find more of Phil's poetry online on his blog:

doggerelbanksy.wordpress.com

Back cover image –

'Casey Jones presents the author with the Best Preserve(d) Cup', photo by Alan Chappell.